An Outline for the Study of Dervishism

Analecta Gorgiana

529

Series Editor
George Anton Kiraz

Analecta Gorgiana is a collection of long essays and short monographs which are consistently cited by modern scholars but previously difficult to find because of their original appearance in obscure publications. Carefully selected by a team of scholars based on their relevance to modern scholarship, these essays can now be fully utilized by scholars and proudly owned by libraries.

An Outline for the Study of Dervishism

Covering Six Elementary Lectures on the
Popular Development of Sufism or
Mohammedan Mysticism

George Swan

gorgias press
2010

Gorgias Press LLC, 954 River Road, Piscataway, NJ, 08854, USA

www.gorgiaspress.com

Copyright © 2010 by Gorgias Press LLC

Originally published in 1925

All rights reserved under International and Pan-American Copyright Conventions. No part of this publication may be reproduced, stored in a retrieval system or transmitted in any form or by any means, electronic, mechanical, photocopying, recording, scanning or otherwise without the prior written permission of Gorgias Press LLC.

2010

ISBN 978-1-61719-190-9   ISSN 1935-6854

Printed in the United States of America

NOTE.

The material which follows comprises the subject matter of six lectures on Dervishism prepared by Mr. George Swan for use in a seminar offered by the School of Oriental Studies of the American University at Cairo. It follows necessarily that, both in form and content, this material must be regarded as subject to revision and further development. For the convenience of students, however, it has been judged an advantage to have in printed form the material that was brought together in connection with the lectures already given. Copies of this pamphlet may be secured through the Secretary of the School of Oriental Studies, 113 Sharia Kasr el Aini, Cairo, Price P.T. 10.

DERVISHISM.

Six Elementary Lectures on the Popular Development of Sufism or Mohammedan Mysticism.

by

George Swan.

The aim of this course of lectures, as of all the courses contemplated by the School of Oriental Studies for missionary students, is not with a view to making them orientalists or even experts in some phase of Mohammedan beliefs or customs, though expert knowledge of this is not to be deprecated for by specializing upon a topic the student may benefit the whole missionary body and help to the greater efficiency of those who seek to bring the gospel effectively to the Mohammedans. The immediate aim is to give the student a few keys whereby he can open the doors of mystery that will confront him at every turn as he seeks to come into sympathetic touch with the mental and actual life of the people among whom he works.

No matter how short a time the student may have been in the country he must have seen many things that have aroused his interest and to which he has sought an explanation. One of the most useful things a new missionary can do is to start from the first a special note book for his own personal observations which might be very suitably called a "Why book". Such a book carefully kept would be of more real educational value than many lectures and the perfunctory reading of many books.

While the Traditions of Mohammed will answer innumerable questions as to the religious customs of the people and even many which we would call secular, Dervishism will be found to be the key to most of what we would term their superstitions. In fact there are two chapters in Lane's *Modern Egyptians*. entitled "Superstitions" that should be read as soon as possible and to which there will be constant reference. These superstitions, many of them very gross, will be found to have their roots in highly philosophical mysticism.

The lecturer has by experience found that students are often very much handicapped by lack of a rudimentary knowledge of Mysticism even in their own religion. The very first opportunity should be taken to remedy this. The most concise introduction to Christian Mysticism known to the lecturer is *An Introduction to Christian Mysticism* by Eleanor C. Gregory (Heart and Life Booklets No. 18. H. R. Allenson, Ltd. London).

It is indispensable that the student should study carefully the *short passages* given at the end of each lecture for reading while it is very advisable to consult the books of reference.

LECTURE 1.
Introductory.

1. *When did Mohammedan Mysticism commence?*

The reply to this question is that it developed contemporaneously with the commencement of Mohammedanism, for mysticism, a word confessedly difficult to define, is, according to Pfleiderer "nothing, therefore, but the fundamental feeling of religion - the religious life at its very heart and center." Undoubtedly there was much of the mystic in Mohammed himself and his life, especially the part connected with his revelations, has always had a most profound effect upon all subsequent developments.

But to understand Mohammedan mysticism one needs to go back to mystic systems prior to Islam, for in all mysticisms there has been first the "fundamental feeling", and this has been followed by a desire to express this feeling in words or to justify it. The discovery that others have trod the same path, and have systematized their experiences has always been welcome and led on to eclecticism or the selecting of opinions from thinkers of other schools of thought and of other religions.

Professor Nicholson in his *Mystics of Islam* gives as the most important external influences on Sufism, the following:

(1) Christianity (2) Neoplatonism (3) Gnosticism (4) Buddhism.

2. *How did Christianity affect Mohammedan mysticism?*

From the very first, men of the more deeply religious type seemed drawn towards the Christian monks; in fact there is a persistent tradition that Mohmmed himself was not free from monkish influence. An interesting side study, about which very little is known as yet is the identity of the Hanifs, vague mentions of whom are to be found in the Koran; the general opinion is that they were pre-Islamic ascetics, very much influenced by the monks of Arabia, and in the opinion of some their effect upon the mind of Mohammed has to be seriously considered when seeking to account for the origin of Islam (See article "Hanif" in *Encyclopedia of Islam.)*

The influence of Christianity is very evident in the earliest Sufi literature. It is astonishing how frequently one comes across references to the words and works of the Lord Jesus Christ; most of them apocryphal as one might expect from what we know of Christianity in Arabia in those days.

3. *How did Neoplatonism affect Mohammedan mysticism.*

To quote from Prof. Nicholson, "Oriental Christian mysticism, however, contained a pagan element; it had long ago absorbed the ideas and adopted the language of Plotinus and the Neoplatonic school."

This opens up for us here in Egypt a most interesting field of origins and it must not be forgotten that Egypt exercised a profound influence on the Sufism of the whole Mohammedan world. We know (1) that Egypt was steeped in Hellenism, at the beginning of the

Christian era and the strong influence on Hellenistic thought caused by the writings of Philo, himself steeped in the teachings of Plato; (2) that the Neoplatonic school resulted from the teachings of his pupils and (3) that it was accompanied by a fever of monasticism later. This is all well worth some study. Very valuable information on this topic will be found in H. A. Vaughan's *Hours with the Mystics.*

One of the most influential of these Neoplatonists who succeeded Plotinus was a man who wrote under the pseudonym of Dionysius the Areopagite. His principal work was translated into Latin by John Scotus Erigena and was the very heart and soul of medieval monasticism as well as of profound influence on the German mystics of the thirteenth and fourteenth centuries. Here then we find one of the chief reasons for the great similarity of terms between Mohammedan mysticism and Christian.

The monastic mystic system of the Neoplatonists was known as that of the Theraputae. A very ancient account of these recluses who lived in communities on the shores of Lake Mariut reads to us extraordinarily like the methods of worship (Zikrs) of dervish orders such as the Rifaiyya. (*See* H. A. Vaughan's *Hours with the Mystics.*)

Later the Nile Valley was full of Christian monks, these monks were saturated with Neoplatonism, a Neoplatonism that soon degenerated in the hands of extremely ignorant monks recruited from the fields of Egypt. Then followed the Moslem invasion and the enforced conversion, in one way or another, of millions of Copts who carried with them into Islam the ideas and traditions which they had learned from the great army of monks that had for so long dominated Egypt. Is it to be wondered that when the Dervish orders were beginning to be formed about the eleventh century, they exactly fitted the tastes of the Mohammedan fellahin whose forbears had helped to people the Nile Valley with monks?

Interwoven with the Neoplatonic chain was the more ancient chain of the Egyptian mysteries, undoubtedly one of the pagan influences to which Prof. Nicholson points. Prof Maspero has no doubt that much of the religious life of the people of Egypt at the present time goes right back to the mysteries; he says of the Tanta Mulid:— "The Mohammedan Egyptians offer the Sheikh Sidi Ahmed el Bedawi the same homage of prayer and disorder as their pagan ancestors gave to Bastit, the cat goddess." (*New Light on Ancient Egypt,* Maspero.)

4. How did Gnosticism affect Mohammedan Mysticism ?

There are many traces of Gnosticism in the beliefs of the Dervishes, among them the quest of the "great name" of God, the discovery of which gives miraculous powers to the finder, also in the belief in the ever-living person "el Khidr. In this connection it is an interesting fact that the parents of Maaruf el Kharka, one of the very earliest writers on Sufism and the author of the earliest definition of the term, were Mandaeans ; a sect of Mesopotamia which sought to synchronize Christianity with various pagan views and had ideas very similar to the Gnostics proper.

The traces of dualism, the separation of the godhead into two, the one a power of good, the other of evil ; the inherent evil of all matter ; the conception of a number of veils between the soul and God, and the ascending scale in nearness to God of a hierarchy of celestial beings, are all to be traced to Gnosticism.

Prof Ramsay has, by his discoveries in Asia Minor, thrown very much light on the beliefs and customs of the early Gnostics and on the relation of the Epistle to the Colossians to them, which ought to make that Epistle more useful to the missionary in combating similar errors held by Moslem Mystics. *(The Contemporary Review*, Aug., 1913, p. 198).

5. *How has Buddhism affected Mohammedan mysticism ?*

Much Buddhist influence has come to Mohammedan mysticism via Persia and Iraq. Prof Goldziher has called attention to the fact that the story of the great Sufi saint, Ibrahim ibn Adham, at one time Prince of Balkh and afterwards a wandering ascetic, is just the story of Buddha over again. Added to this there were great Buddhist monasteries in Balkh in the days of the great growth of Sufism and many of the prominent Sufis dwelt there. The Sufi doctrine of el-Fana, literally destruction, but technically meaning absorption into God, corresponds with the Buddhist "Nirvana". Sufism has, however, its positive side "el Baqa" which means everlasting life in God. The use of the "Sibha" (rosary) is borrowed from Buddhism as are also many of their practices for the inducement of contemplation and ecstasy. But when it comes to matters of principle Prof. Nicholson asserts that Buddhism and Sufism are poles apart.

6. *The Koran and Mohammedan mysticism.*

We have stated that the life of Mohammed has profoundly affected Mohammedan mysticism but it owes very little indeed to the Koran or even the traditions excepting insofar as these reveal the inner life of Mohammed himself. There are a few verses in the Koran which express a real aspiration after a full knowledge of God, but they are very few indeed. They give, however, to the Sufi sufficient excuse to interpret the Koran in the light of his systematized mysticism. Some of these interpretations very much recall the allegorical methods of interpretation of the early fathers of Alexandria.

7. *Mohammed in mysticism and Orthodoxy.*

One of the marvels of Islam is the acceptance, by the Orthodox school, of the Sufis with their doctrines, seemingly entirely antagonistic to all the teaching of the Schoolmen. At one time they were persecuted even to the point of being put to death for their views. The God of the Scholastics, for example, is more of a transcendental abstraction than that of the Koran, whilst the God of the Sufi is immanent to the degree of extreme pantheism. And yet this mysticism has been accepted as an integral part of Islam by "Igma'a" that is, the catholic consent of the people of Islam. That brilliant scholar, philosopher and Sufi, el Ghazzali, had much to do in thus reconciling the two. The process by which he and many other brilliant writers accomplished this seems to us to have been by categorical denial of the reality of appearances, that the flagrantly unorthodox doings and sayings of the reputed saint were only unorthodox in appearance not in reality. They were at great pains to explain apparent discrepancies of doctrine and practice; however far these acts and sayings were removed from the teaching and example of Mohammed and his followers. An example of this kind of argument is indicated in the Koran. (Sura The Cave (18) vv. 64-81. The commentators telling us that the instructor of Moses was el-Khidr.)

For Reading ; -

Lane's *Modern Egyptians* Chapters X and XI.

Koran Sura "The Cave" vv. 64—81.

For Reference :—

Gregory's *An Introduction to Christian Mysticism.*

Lehman's *Mysticism in Christendom and Heathendom,* translated by G. M. Hunt.

Nicholson's *The Mystics of Islam.*

Maspero's *New Light on Ancient Egypt.*

Vaughan's *Hours with the Mystics.*

LECTURE II.
Beginnings.

In the previous lecture we considered the external sources from which Mohammedan mysticism borrowed. We are now to consider the growth and development of mystical teaching in Islam itself leading up to that great popular movement that culminated in the foundation of the dervish orders.

1. The Development from Fear. Professor Nicholson shows how the predominating feature of the Moslem religion, during the eighth century was fear of God, fear of Hell, fear of death and fear of sin". He says the earliest Sufis were in fact, ascetics and quietists rather than mystics. An overwhelming consciousness of sin, combined with a dread—which it is hard for us to realize of Judgment day and of the torments of hell fire, so vividly painted in the Koran, drove them to seek salvation in flight from the world. On the other hand, the Koran warned them that salvation depended entirely on the inscrutable will of Allah who guides aright the good and leads astray the wicked. Their fate was inscribed in the eternal tables of His providence, nothing could alter it. Only this was sure, that if they were destined to be saved by fasting and praying and pious work—then they would be saved. Such a belief ends naturally in quietism, complete and unquestioning submission to the divine will, an attitude characteristic of Sufism in its oldest form. (Nicholson's *Mystics of Islam, p. 4*) Professor Nicholson goes on to show how the woman saint Rabi'a introduced the element of "truly mystical self-abandonment". In the ninth century he says "they began to regard asceticism as only the first stage of a long journey—the preliminary training for a larger spiritual life than the mere ascetic is able to conceive". (*Ibid p. 6*). "These ideas," he says, "light, knowledge and love form, as it were, the keynotes of the new Sufism . . . . : ultimately they rest upon a pantheistic faith which deposed the One Transcendent God of Islam and worshipped in his stead One Real Being who dwells and works everywhere, and whose throne is not less, but more, in the human heart than in the heaven of heavens. (*Ibid p. 8*)

2. The Development of the Creed.

Another book that treats of the development of Mohammedan Sufism from a somewhat different angle though agreeing with the ascetic beginnings, is the "*Early Development of Mohammedanism*" by Margoliouth. The student is especially advised to read Chapters V and VI. His Chapter V is to a considerable extent founded on material collected from one of the earliest Sufi books, the "*Qut el Qulub*" of Abu Talib el-Makki. Professor Margoliouth shows in Chapter V that the early Mohammedan ascetic "was occupied with exaggeration of the four performances enjoined by Islam. We shall now find him developing unlooked-for consequences from the primary proposition of the system there is no God but Allah with whom nothing must be associated : . . . If God is to be loved then nothing else may be loved; no other object of affection would be associated with God, and the person who bestowed the affection would be a pagan. The same argument excludes all desires : if the worshipper's object is paradise, then he is desiring something besides God, and so is a polytheist . . . . The cultivation of poverty, humilation and resignation belong to the negative aspect of the first proposition of the creed; if the word "God" signifies an object of attachment then the ascetic who follows the discipline which has been sketched has clearly severed bonds which ordinarily attach men to other things than God ; but there is also the positive side of the proposition to be considered and this is summed up in the phrase "love of God" . . . . Love of God is not only incompatible with the bestowal of affection on other rational beings, but even with the most innocent enjoyments. In a revelation to Moses, fault was found with a man who was perfect in every other respect, but enjoyed the morning air . . . . But besides the moral conclusions to be drawn from the doctrine of Divine unity, there is also a metaphysical conclusion; and this appears to be the extreme attainment of the *Gnosis* . . . . The true unitarian is he who recognizes in the world no existence save God's : who regards both himself and the world outside him as a mirror, yet rather one wherein the Deity shows himself than one where He is reflected. The mirror is the soul *inside of which* is the image of God, as distinct as the mirror is clear and pure.

3. *Outstanding names in the History of Mohammedan Mysticism.*

There are certain names to which reference is constantly made in Sufi books of the Dervish orders. A systematic study of these would probably prove extremely fruitful in arriving at an under standing of the development of Mohammedan Mysticism. The difficulty is to get authentic information. The oriental is not a historian much less a writer of biography. Sha'arani, one of the ablest defenders of the dervish orders, and a voluminous writer, has a famous book called "*Et Tabaqat el Kubra*", which is supposed to be an account of all Mohammedan saints from the time of Mohammed to about the middle of the tenth century of the Moslem era. The amount of biography in these two volumes of 162 and 154 pages would probably not fill ten pages, the bulk of the matter being the supposed sayings of the saints. A small book in English by Claud Field entitled "*The Saints of Islam*" should be read by the student.

The names of those about whom the student should collect as much information as he can are :—

Hassan el Basri who was born in the year 19 A.H. in Medina; he lived to a great age, dying in 110 A. H. He was a great fearless teacher and ascetic; the fear of God and humility were his chief characteristics. All Sufi writers quote him freely and probably a very large volume could be compiled of sayings reputed to him in books not long subsequent to his time. Curiously enough he is left out of Sha'arani's *Tabaqat el Kubra*, probably because he is left out of the *Risala* of el Qushairi, one of the oldest authorities on Sufism.

Rabi'a el Addawiya, the woman saint, who died in 134 A.H., is one of the great characters in Mohammedan Mysticism. She had been in touch with Hassan el Basri. The theme of disinterested love had a large place in her teaching. Sha'arani says she was much given to weeping, the place of her devotions being like a bog from her many tears. One of her sayings quoted by him is "our seeking of forgiveness needs seeking of forgiveness."

Ibrahim ibn Adham, who died in the year 261 A. H., was the son of a Prince, Sulaiman Adham ibn Mansur, who resigned his throne and became a dervish. Passing through Balkh he became enamoured of the daughter of the Sultan. After miraculous experiences they were married and lived as recluses. Ibrahim was born. After his mother's death, his father took him to Balkh for his education. He was recognized by his grandmother and eventually became a prince of Balkh. After many indications of the Divine call he left his kingdom and became a wandering Dervish. As stated in the previous lecture, Goldziher considers the story of Ibn Adham as fictitious and merely an adapation of the life of Buddha, but there seems considerable evidence on the side of his having been a historical character. He often prayed: "O God, uplift me from the shame of disobedience to the glory of submission to thee".

Dhu-el-Nun (Quranic name for Jonah i. e. he of the fish) was a Nubian saint born at Akhmim in Upper Egypt. He died at Gizeh in the year 245 A. H. He is said to have had great influence on Egyptian mysticism, though he seems to have been more quoted by Jalal-el-Din Rumi, the great Turkish mystic and poet, than by Arab Sufi writers. He probably, however, greatly influenced the populace, it being recorded that immense crowds attended his funeral. The learned had him arraigned for heresy, which was the fate of many of the early mystics. We have already stated that he was saturated with Neoplatonic thought.

El-Juneid, who died in 297 A, H. was a scholarly mystical teacher who is constantly quoted in Sufi books. He made the pilgrimage from Mesopotamia to Mecca on foot 50 times. He had a school of mystics in Baghdad which created a big stir and much opposition from Scholastic theologians. One of his most quoted sayings is "Water is the colour of its vessel":

Shibli, his pupil, who died in 334 A. H. was the poet of el Juneid's school. His beautiful sayings constantly quoted must have had a powerful influence in his day. (For Shibli and other writers and poets of the mystics, see Nicholson's *Literary History of the Arabs)*. Nicholson in *Mystics of Islam* gives an interesting account of his training in the Sufi way by Juneid (pp. 34 & 35). One of Shibli's expressions in prayer was "Men have loved thee for thy good things but I love thee for thine afflictions".

Al Hallaj was martyred in 309 A. H. He carried El-Juneid's teaching to its logical conclusion fearlessly and enthusiastically, and suffered martyrdom for saying "I am the truth". His death must have had a consolidating effect upon Sufism, leading on to vigorous apologetics, and the apparent reconciliation of Sufi doctrines with the orthodox Islam of the schools, by men of the type of el-Qushairi who died in 465 A. H., and that perhaps greatest of Mohammedan learned men, el Ghazzali, who died in 405 A. H.

4. To fill in the period that intervened between the great schools of mysticism in Baghdad such as that of el-Juneid and the great popular movement that led to the formation of the Dervish Orders is not difficult, for we have many accounts of the lives of the saints of that period. One that is especially helpful in this respect is *El-Mathir el-Shadhaliya*, being an account of the order of the Shadhaliya, an order much favoured by the Azhar. We get a picture of the aspirants after *Gnosis* travelling from one saint to another. El Shadhali travelled from Morocco to Iraq asking for the *Qutb*, the Pole or Chief of all saints and there was told that the Qutb was near his own home in Morocco and travelled back there. Afterwards as a great saint himself, he traversed the whole of North Africa many times on pilgrimages to Mecca and at all the places where he stopped you get pictures of the crowds sitting at his feet for teaching, wondering at his mighty powers, and in the case of the most earnest seeking to follow in his footsteps. There must have been very large numbers of these saints in every town of the Moslem world and most of them often travelling. In fact a vast number of contemporaries are mentioned in the above book and one realizes what a wonderful unity the far extended Moslem world was in those days, in spite of the lack of trains and steamships.

For Reading :—

    Claud Field's *"The Saints of Islam"*.

    Margoliouth's *"The Early Development of Mohammedanism.*
        Chapter V & VI

    Nicholson's *"The Literary History of the Arabs.* Chapter V.
                                                               pp. 224 - 34.

    The Confessions of Ghazzali. Chapter VIII. pp. 379–404.

N. B. The *Risala* of el Qushairi should be noted for reading with an Arabic teacher at an early date ; care being taken that the teacher is one who knows something of Sufism, otherwise the technicalities will puzzle him. If the Library contains a translation it should be read in the meantime.

For Reference :—

    La Passion d'al-Hallaj, by L. Massignon.

    Kashf el Mahjub, translated by Nicholson.

LECTURE III.
Dervish Orders: Organisation.

The use of the word "Orders" is purely western and taken from its use in monasticism because of the great similarity of the two organisations. The Arabic word is "el Turuq" i. e. the ways; singular "el Tariqa" meaning the way to mystical union with God.

We have already seen how there was never a time in the history of Islam without some men or women standing out notably from the great mass of believers on account of their more intense devotion. The reputation of their saintliness was carried to the furthest confines of the Arabic conquests, and those souls who longed for a more satisfying spiritual experience than traditional Mohammedanism could give them, gathered around these men as pupils to learn from them the secret of their saintly lives. We have seen how Mesopotamia led the way in these "Schools of the Prophets" but it was not long before their pupils, some of whom travelled from the ends of the Mohammedan world, returned to their own countries and set up similar schools. As these pupils travelled backwards and forwards they spread the knowledge of the teachings of these saints in all the cities, towns and villages through which they passed.

1. *The Four Aqtab.*

It will be convenient to take the foundation of the Dervish Orders as stated by themselves, without going critically into their real beginnings.

The word "Qutb" (pl. Aqtab) literally means pole or axis and is primarily given to the supreme living saint of any time though all notable saints are given it as a courtesy title and Abd-el-Qadr el Jilani, Ahmed el Rifai, Ahmed el Bedawi and Ibrahim el Dissuki are given it as recognized founders of the Dervish orders.

Of these four, Abd-el-Qadr el-Jilani is more especially considered the originator. It would appear that the reason for this statement is that Abd el-Qadr was so successful as a teacher that the movement under him ceased to be merely a school of thought and became a great popular movement. Tradition has surrounded Abd el-Qadr with a mass of miracles, but it is not difficult to get at the real man from the almost contemporaneous accounts which still exist, and from his sermons; these are considered the best of their kind in the whole range of Mohammedan homiletic literature. They are remarkably sane and we have accounts of a very large school of disciples that gathered round him. This so increased that no place within the walls of Baghdad was large enough for him and he had to hold the school in a specially constructed building outside the gates. He lived to a great old age. To conduct this school successfully would most certainly entail organization and we know that after his death most of his 39 sons became leaders of this movement and lived in the light and privileges of their father's sanctity. We can well imagine how this successful movement in Baghdad became a model for other similar movements in all parts of the Mohammedan world. The character of the organization we will see later.

Ahmed el-Rifa'i seems to have been the St. Francis of the Dervish orders. He saw God in the fields around him. He was wonderfully kind to all animals, and would kill none, not even the vermin upon his person. He was a man of great humility: he kissed the hands and feet of those who abused him. He was however more of an ecstatic than Abd el-Qadr. His love of animals would probably lead to a certain power over them and it is not unlikely that he had other powers of an hypnotic order which were the result of his contemplative and ecstatic life. However this may be, miraculous power over animals, especially snakes, is attributed to him, and I think that there can be no doubt, making a large allowance for trickery, that his followers to-day have a very real power over these reptiles.

Ahmed el-Bedawi was a man of entirely different calibre. He was a Moroccan brought to Mecca in his boyhood. He was wild and careless, a great horseman, hence his name el-Bedawi. Like most great Sufis he had a spiritual crisis when about 30 years of age, after which he renounced his former life, visited the tombs of Abd el-Qadr and Ahmed el-Rifa'i and entirely gave himself over to a life of contemplation. Visions played a leading part in his life, and it was in obedience to a vision that he came to Egypt, found his way to Tantah and made his first appearance there on a roof. Gazing up into the sun and occasionally giving vent to great screams; he continued thus for days, until his eyes swelled and became a flaming red. He soon attracted followers who became his pupils and imitated him in his forms of ecstacy and were at first known as Roofists. Ahmed el-Bedawi was neither intellectually nor morally great. He was a man of the Yogi type, yet in his lifetime he seems to have brought all Egypt to his feet, including the great Sultan Baibars.

There seems to be little doubt that his coming fitted in with the long latent beliefs of the people that still held much of the old Egyptian mysteries connected with sun worship and the rise and fall of the Nile, his festivals synchronising with these latter and not with the Mohammedan calendar.

Ibrahim el-Dissuki seems to have exerted an influence in Egypt through his power of speaking in tongues. There are still books extant with pages of matter taken down by his pupils from the lips of Dissuki when he was speaking in an unknown tongue. It is a curious fact that much of this old tongues movement was similar to the extravagant tongues movements that have found some vogue in America and England during recent years, and it is not difficult to prove that the errors in both cases have similar causes.

2. *The Organization with respect to Order.*

It has often been said that in Islam there is nothing equivalent to an organised Christian clergy. This is certainly true of scholastic Islam ; but it is far from true with regard to the Dervish orders.

We have seen that most of the Dervish orders attribute their origin to one of the four Aqtab :—

    Abd el-Qadir el-Jilani
    Ahmed el-Rifa'i
    Ahmed el-Badawi
    Ibrahim el-Dissuki

Each of these orders has several branch orders, but with most of them the headship of the order is hereditary, The living head of the order is called Sheikh el-Sigada; the word "Sigada" meaning ordinarily a prayer-mat, but in this case the sheepskin, which is the Dervish throne, and generally supposed to be the particular one on which the head of the order sat. This Sheikh el-Sigada has a substitue called the Wakil Sheikh el-Sigada.

He has also four henchmen, the nuqaba. Gehazi in the Old Testament seems typical of these Nuqaba. Then in every village or town or hamlet there are representatives of the Sheikh el-Sigada who are called " Khulafa " (Singular " Khalifa "). Those who remember the Mahdi rising in the Sudan will remember that after the death of the Mahdi the dervishes were still led by one named Abdullahi who was known as the Khalifa, for he represented the Mahdi or was his vicar. In large towns where it is advisable to subdivide, there are several Khulafa, but in such cases there is one who is recognized as the head and called the Khalifat-el Khulafa. Then come the Akhwan or brethren of the order.

It will be readily understood then, how easy it is for an order from the Sheikh el Sigada to pass to the humblest member of the through the Sheikh's representatives and their subordinates. That completes the earthly hierarchy.

3. *The Organization with respect to Faith.*

There is a heavenly hierarchy, of this we shall speak later ; but in every order there are some others who play a prominent part though not that of Government. The most prominent of these latter is the " 'Am ". This word in Arabic means Uncle and in the Dervish idiom is a title of high respect. Nearly every Khalifa is also an "'Am", but one may be an 'Am without being a Khalifa. The Sheikh el Sigada, though head of the mystic order, may himself be far from mystical. He may, in fact, be, as he often is, a far going infidel holding the office simply because of his family right; but the 'Am must know how to initiate into the order : it is he that is responsible for taking hold of the raw ignorant youth and leading him in the way. The would-be initiate is called "Murid" which word implies his desire to know God. All Dervish books are full of the importance of the office of 'Am. At the end of a Bayumi devotional book, I discovered the following directions :— "The Prophet of God has said that he who belittles his Sheikh, his tongue will be enfeebled and he will come to poverty". And in one version of the tradition it says he will die a non-Moslem. Therefore three things are necessary to the Murid. Now the three things that are necessary to the 'Am are, firstly, the causing to enter the beginning (of the Sufi road to God); secondly, the causing to obtain the goal; thirdly, guarding and shepherding the flock. But the three things that are essential to the Murid with regard to his Sheikh are, firstly, obedience to his orders; secondly, the keeping of his secret; thirdly, the magnifying of his estate.

One would expect then to find those who hold the office of 'Am, an office equivalent to "le directeur" of Roman Catholic mysticism, men of intelligence, men of some dignity, leaders of men in fact : and such we come across in many accounts of Moslem mysticism and such are still to be met with to-day in Egypt, but the vast majority are degraded to the last degree. Once when talking to a donkey boy who owned to being a member of a Dervish order, and when I had mentioned some of the simpler teachings of the Dervish orders, of which he confessed his ignorance even of the very terms, I asked him what his 'Am taught him, if not these things. His reply was "the 'Am teaches me nothing, he cares about nothing but to receive his quarter of a pound of coffee or beans or his half a pound of rice". The boy referred to the support of the 'Am which is given to him by his disciples. These are called "awāid" (dues) and every member of an order is expected to pay them to the 'Am. One naturally wonders how such careless leaders can get anything from their disciples, and as a matter of a fact there is great slackness in their payment, but they receive sufficient to live upon, and they mostly do this by playing on the superstition of the people. Most of them have a reputation for magic practices, and it is the fear of this magic on the one hand, and the desire to have it used on their behalf, on the other hand, that gives these men their following.

In the previous lecture we called attention to the story of Moses' encounter with el-Khidr. Here is one of the popular developments of this story as told by Lane in his chapter on Superstitions. I merely summarize it from his *Modern Egyptians*. A devout Cairo merchant was anxious for the post of Sahb el Darak (a kind of supernatural sighted watchman over the interests of the Moslems), being appointed by the Qutb, he took up his duties in the Darb el Ahmar.

The first thing he did was to take up a large stone and smash in pieces, a large jar, containing boiled beans, scattering the contents. The merchant owning them gave the "wali" a mighty beating but afterwards discovered in the bottom of the jar, which remained, a venomous serpent.

The next day he broke a large jar of milk and again received a tremendous thrashing, but the ower of the boiled beans intervened, telling the man that he was thrashing a wali, and advising him to look into what remained of his jar and he would find something either poisonous or unclean. He looked and found the carcass of a dog.

The following day he placed his stick between the legs of a slave carrying a large tray of eatables on his head for a picnic party in the country. The slave wreaked his vengeance on him with a will until one of the bystanders called his attention to the fact that a dog who had partaken of some of the fallen food had died at once. Then he was recognized as a wali, but he did not appreciate his task, and asked to be relieved of his recently acquired honour.

El Dabagh in the book "*Al Ibrīz*" gives very many instances to prove that the Murīd (aspirant Gnosis) can never judge his Sheikh by the sight of his eyes. The essentials of a Murid are that he should submit himself entirely to his Sheikh, trust him implicitly, and jealously guard his "secret". These points are all supposed to be tested. In El Dabagh's stories the various Murids being tested are supposed to see the Sheikhs not only in situations that are grossly compromising but actually "in flagrante delicto" but it is only their faithfulness to their 'Am that is being tested by what they think they see. The stories themselves are vile and show how hellish is the system and how subtly contrived to enslave the souls of men.

The Heavenly Hierarchy.

In addition to the visible rulers of the orders there is a vast hierarchy of invisible rulers. In fact it is the unseen rulers of the Dervish Orders who, in their opinion, also rule the world. The idea of God's "hidden ones" being the actual rulers of the world is one which one meets again and again in all mystical teachings whether Christian, Pagan, or Moslem, and no doubt there is a great truth in the belief, but in Moslem mysticism, it is pushed to an absurd extreme. Every Dervish saint from the days of the Prophet himself, in their opinion, peoples the air around them or may be invoked from the utmost part of the earth or even of the heavens.

Every night in the realm above the earth there is a parliament of these saints (Aulia) in which are present not only the departed saints, but also many of the living saints, and all the affairs of the world are then settled, courts and parliaments on the following day merely carrying out, whether they know it or not, the decisions of this heavenly parliament. Four of these saints are called Autād, a word which signifies "tent-pegs" and to each of them is delegated one of the four corners of the earth. The word "Qutb" means pole, probably of similar purport to the word "autad", the axis round which the government of the world revolves.

At every Mulid there is a pole, in the centre of the Mulid ground called the Sâri. In many towns this pole is a permanent fixture and is erected and kept in repair by the Government. Around this, upon the Mulid, the local departed saints congregate, accompanied by this vast hierarchy of invisible saints, and around it the principal exercises of the dervish, the zikrs, take place.

The chief of the hierarchy is called "Qutb". As far as I can make out the Qutb is always a living saint but with extraordinary powers with regard to movement from place to place. In other words the Qutb may be present in bodily form or only spiritually ; not only so, but may appear to be present in bodily form in two distant places at the same time. This I believe is not the exclusive privilege of the Qutb. In one town a man received recognition as a saint, because pilgrims from Mecca on their return to the town, testified to the fact that on a certain date, when he was known to have been seen in this Egyptian town they had seen him and spoken to him in Mecca. The whole question of the Qutb is a difficult one to understand, but it has a very definite place in the popular mind, especially in Egypt, for two of the favourite haunts of the Qutb are to be found in this country, the Bab el Zuweila in Cairo, and the roof of Ahmed el Bedawi's Mosque at Tantah. Any day and any hour of the day that you visit the Bab el Zuweila, you will find people making their prayers to the unseen Qutb, in the hope that he is present at the time they offer these prayers. The ironwork of the gate is covered with rags, bits of hair, human teeth and other things taken from the body of the person for whom a favour is sought. Women come there with their sick babies and after praying, will rub their hands over the gate and then rub over the child with the idea of obtaining the saint's favour and blessing.

Childless women come there seeking for children. A Dervish is always to be found standing near the door who professes to have the mind of the saint, and these poor people will go to him, put a little money in his hand, and ask him what hope there is that they may have their petitions granted.

People with tooth-ache come and, to remind the Sheikh of the tooth that is causing the trouble, they pull it out and push it into a crevice of the iron-work. The immediate relief, of course is attributed to the saint. Men and women with every kind of request come there. In fact few there be of poorer class that pass that gate without stopping with some request, or at least to say a "fataha" (the opening chapter of the Koran) in favour of the saint.

There seems to be very little doubt that the Moslems inherited *all this* idea of a saintly hierarchy from the angelic hierarchy of the early Gnostics who thought that they could only reach God, "through ranks and ranks of angels," and St. Paul in his epistle to the Colosssians takes pains to show them how they can reach God directly through our Lord Jesus Christ, in whom dwelleth all the fullness of the Godhead bodily.

The following extract, slightly abbreviated, is the verbal account of the heavenly parliament of saints before mentioned, as taken down from the lips of a Moroccan saint, named Abd el Aziz Dabagh, by one of his pupils, Ahmed ibn Mubarak and appears in the book known as *Al-Ibriz.*

"The Parliament is at the cave of Hira where the Prophet used to fly from idolatry and sin before his commission as Prophet.

The GHAWTH* sits outside the cave with Mecca behind his right shoulder and Medina in front of his left knee, having four Qutbs of the Malaki sect on his right hand, and three Qutbs on his left hand, of the other three orthodox sects. Before him sits the Proxy who is called the Judge of the Parliament. At this present time he is also of the Malaki sect, Sidi Mohammed ben Abd el Karim of Basra. With him the Ghawth talks and for this reason he is called the Proxy, for he speaks on behalf of all present in parliament.

The executive is in the hands of the seven Qutbs under the Command of the Ghawth. Each of the seven Qutbs has under him a certain number of executive officers. There are six rows behind the Proxy in the form of a circle from the fourth Qutb on the right to the third Qutb on the left, the seven Qutbs completing the first circle, the second row is behind and concentric with the first, then the third and fourth until you come to the sixth.

A few women are present in three rows near the three Qutbs on the left of the Ghawth.

Some of the perfected dead also attend and are mingled in the ranks of the living but are distinguishable by three things: (1) Unchangeableness, in distinction to the living whose beard and hair are sometimes trimmed and their clothes changed. (2) They never counsel in matters concerning the living for they have no authority in them but matters concerning the dead were referred to them. For this reason when one visits the tombs and wants to plead with God through one of His Saints, as intermediary on behalf of one of the dead, there will be a greater likehood of success if a dead saint be the intermediary. (3) The third distinctive feature of these saints is that they have no shadow, the reason being that he is present in his spiritual self, not his corruptible earthly self, and the spirit is light, not heavy; transparent, not opaque.

Many a time (says Dabagh who describes this Parliament) when I have been present at the Parliament or one of the meetings of the

---

* The distinguishing title of the great "Qutb"

saints, and the sun has arisen, they have seen me from afar and greeted me and I have seen them with my own eyes distinguishing this one by his shadow, and that one by the absence of shadow.

These dead saints, when they attend the Parliament, descend from El-Barzakh (the place of departed saintly spirits), flying with spiritual flight, but when they come near to the place of meeting they descend to the earth and walk upon their feet out of respect to the living and from fear of them. So also is it with those men who have the power of passing out of their bodies and of moving in an angelic condition from place to place, for when one of these visits another he descends to the ground and walks in his corporeal body out of respect and from fear.

The angels also attend and stand behind the rows, the perfect ones from among the Jinns also attend, they are the spiritual ones and stand behind all; they do not complete a whole row. The reason for the presence of the angels is this. The saints carry out everything that is in their power, but for those things that are beyond their power they call in the help of the angels and Jinns. Sometimes the Prophet attends the gathering and when he does so, he takes the place of the Ghawth, and the Ghawth takes the place of the Proxy and the Proxy goes back to a row. If the Prophet attends, there come with him those lights that cannot be described save that they burn and terrify and kill instantly ; the lights of awe and majesty and power. If we could conceive of forty men of limitless courage coming suddenly upon these lights they would shriek with terror. God, however, has granted His saints power to meet them, but few of these can grasp the orders promulgated in the hour when he is present. When present the Prophet speaks with the Ghawth, when he is absent the Ghawth also has wonderful lights so that none of those present can approach near to him but sit at some distance from him.

The Prophet comes from the presence of God when the matter in hand is beyond the power of the Ghawth.

The hour of the gathering is the hour of the night in which the Prophet was born. It is the hour of answering, the hour when our Lord descends to the heaven of the earth each night there remains but a third of the night, the hour, when, according to the traditions, our Lord says, "he who asks shall receive".

If anyone wishes to succeed in presenting his petition at this hour, let him repeat when he wishes to sleep the Sura that commences "Verily they that believe and do good works to them are the gardens of paradise" to the end of the Sura. Two believers in the *same room* have been known to wake up at the same moment by this method.

This parliament was first constituted of angels, then when God sent the Prophet it was constituted of the saints of this people (the Moslems) so apparently the angels represented the saints until this glorious people appeared. As the saints received their saintship they took their places one by one in the rows, and as they did so the angel who previously occupied the seat rose and flew away, and so until the number of saints was completed. The angels standing at the back are the special attendants of the Prophet.

In every town there are a number of angels (about seventy, sometimes more, sometimes less) who are there to help the executive saints in the things that are beyond each one's power. These angels are present in each town in human form, sometimes they are met in the form of a Christian merchant, sometimes in that of a beggar, and other times in that of a little child. They are mixed up amongst the people who are unaware of their presence.

For Reading :—
    Macdonald's   *Aspects of Islam*—Lecture V.
          ,,   *The Religious Attitude and Life in Islam.*
                        Lecture I-pp. 1 to 11
                              ,, VI—pp.157-165

For Reference :—
    Depont and Coppolani's *Confréries Religieuses Musulmanes".*

LECTURE IV.

Dervish Orders : Worship.

We come now to consider the methods of worship of these orders and the first point to be noted is how a man enters an order.

1. *Initiation.* (Arabic, talqin). We need not spend much time on this subject other than refer the student to several accounts of initiation that have been fully given. There is the classical account given by Tawakkul Beg in the *Journal Asiatique* and quoted in many works on Mohammedanism. It is to be found in Hughes *Dictionary of Islam* p. 121 (and in the preceding two columns a more general account of talqin is given) and Sell's *Faith of Islam* page 135 et seq. (This account is followed by an interesting account of Umar Khayyam): A local account of the Dimerdashiya Order is given by Lane in his *Modern Egyptians*, p. 252.

In practice many of the teachers in the Moslem schools (kuttab, pl, katatib) are Dervishes who initiate the youths under them, or if they do not, their schools are frequently visited by Dervishes who do.

It remains to be said that a prime necessity of initiation is an a   te submission of spirit, soul and body to the 'Am or Sheikh ᴠ   itiates. There is very much of this in Dervish books.

2. *Classified capacity of the Murid, or candidate.* The adaptation of Sufism to the varying capacities of men is illuminatingly stated in the *Ma'athir el Shadhaliya* :—

"Sheikh Abd-el-Wathid-Maghrabi-el-Mutatabbib in his essay on the Way, mentions that the Way is divided into three divisions and that men according to their different conditions may also be divided into three divisions, to each one a Way peculiar to him: (a) Those who are of a heavy build and dull in their understanding, who find it almost impossible to find education, and who cannot understand the greater niceties of speech. Their way is that of Worship and asceticism through much fasting and prayer and reading of the Quran and pilgrimage and jihad: (holy fighting) and other outward works. For this class, on account of their physical strength, their powerful limbs, and the strength of their heart, are able to bear a severe worship without weariness but rather they become easily accustomed to it. Those who walk in this way continue in these methods climbing up the ladder until their dullness is lightened and they begin to approach unto the condition that is capable of receiving knowledge, and then the praises of the Beloved One are revealed to them and they see the wonder of the unseen, and their inner man is enlarged to understand what their minds cannot grasp. BUT THIS WAY IS IMMENSELY DIFFICULT AND THOSE WHO ATTAIN BY ITS MEANS ARE ONLY INDIVIDUALS

(b) Those who are of quick understanding and of choice character, whose bodily temples are full of light and whose spirits are exalted like those of high rank, yet those who are confused by intellectual doubts and who are unable to curb their tempers. Their Way consists in religious efforts and exercises, in improving their characters, in purifying their souls, and striving towards the cultivation of the inner life. Those who walk in this way continue to make effort to erase those evil characteristics that are inherent in their souls until they restore it to its original purity. The way to accomplish this is by opposing its lusts and refusing its desires until good-will and anger, rest and effort, or the absence of it, descent to the lowest of ranks, profit and the loss of him who gives up every profession and means of livlihood, become one and the same thing to him; such a man has saved his soul from its evils with a perfect salvation, he has become worthy of receiving into his soul the ultimate truths and to attempt to walk in the way of the choice souls. THIS WAY AS COMPARED WITH THAT WHICH PRECEDED IS A WAY OF TERRORS AND THOSE WHO HAVE ATTAINED HAVE BEEN THE MOST EMINENT OF MEN BUT WITH REGARD TO NUMBERS THERE ARE MORE OF THEM THAN THOSE WHO HAVE WALKED THE WAY OF ACTS OF WORSHIP AND THEY TAKE LESS TIME TO ACCOMPLISH THE JOURNEY AND THOSE WHO HAVE ATTAINED ARE VERY GREAT AND FAMED MURSHIDS (Leader).

(c) Those who possess a soul God satisfied, an enlightened mind, and righteous disposition, whose bodies are perfectly pure, well balanced and well favoured. Their Way is the way of those that hasten to God, nay those that fly to him; they are the people of love who proceed to God by attraction (Gadhb). The method to accomplish this is by the purifying of the heart, the perfecting of love, and the ascertaining inwardly and outwardly of the obligations of trust in God; he must then forsake his own might and power; his wisdom and intelligence, until, if asked to spill his own life blood he would find no difficulty; then there is inbreathed in him the very spirit of vision, and all who have perception perceive the truth of his words. THIS WAY IS THE VERY PERFECTION OF EASE ON ACCOUNT OF ITS VOTARIES WHO ARE BETROTHED TO ITS GLORIOUS UNION AND IT IS POSSIBLE FOR THE PILGRIM IN THIS WAY TO ATTAIN IN A BREATH AND TO OUTSTRIP HIM WHO SEEKS TO PURIFY HIMSELF BY EFFORT AND STUDY.

All of these three ways and those that are derived from them are desirable, but some are harder and longer and some easier and shorter, and if the Sheikh understands the treatment of the soul's diseases and is proficient in diagnosing its characteristics and its failings he will cause some of every class to walk in a plain and certain way and will restore the ways of righteousness. For human souls are a mirror to the divine light of revelation, and according to its dullness or corrosion he prescribes for its cleansing and polishing; so forbear to threaten and be harsh, for truth is nearer than the jugular vein. I have said and it is self-evident that the Shadhaliya is the third of these ways.

3. The Classification of the Soul. The Dervish orders almost universally speak of the seven souls, the object (of the exercises prescribed to the Murid by his Sheikh) being to lead him on step by step from the lowest kind of soul to the highest. The seven souls are:

    The Soul Depraved (el Nafsu-l-Ammara b-is-su)
    The Soul Accusatory (el Nafsu-l-Lawwama)
    The Soul Inspired (el Nafsu-l-Mulhama)
    The Soul Tranquil (el Nafsu-l-Mutma'inna)
    The Soul God-Satisfied (el Nafsu-el-Radija)
    The Soul God Satisfying (el Nafsu-l-Mardija)
    The Soul clarified (el Nafsu-l-Safija) or the Perfect Soul (el-Nafsu-l-Kamila).

A description of these seven souls and their treatment is to be found in the two articles by Canon Gairdner in the *Moslem World.* Vol II., entitled "The Way of a Mohammedan Mystic." These articles were taken down by Canon Gairdner from the mouth of two Mohammedans he met in Germany. The Canon wonders if we have not in this "a doctrine of which the lower grades are entirely ignorant". I may say that I possessed at the time of the appearance of these articles a small and very cheap Arabic book that was so close to the Canon's articles that it would seem that his two informants had this book off by heart even to the excellent table given at the end of the article; the inference being that the information is available for the rank and file, and my observation goes to show that the ignorant classes are the greatest purchasers and readers of such books.

4. The Zikr, or the Treatment of the Soul. It will have been noted by a perusal of Canon Gairdner's article that the Zikr is the chief instrument in the purifying of the soul and it is as varied as the states of a man's soul are varied.

The word Zikr means remembrance; technically it means the remembrance of God. The Sufi finds his authority for the use of the Zikr in the Quran in the chapter called "the Spider" v. 44. "Recite that which has been revealed to thee of the book and perform prayer, for prayer restraineth from the filthy and the *blameworthy* and the most important duty is the remembrance of God". It need hardly be said that Mohammed had no such thing in mind as the Zikrs of the Dervish orders when he gave this text as having been revealed to him by God, but we may see in this passage some insight into the principle that was so emphasised by Brother Lawrence, *"The Practice of the Presence of God"*, and of that which was crystalized by Dr A. J. Gordon in the sentence "the expulsive power of a new affection". There is something of this idea in the Zikr of the Dervishes but exaggerated to an absurd degree and with the masses becoming a mere orgy of extreme excitement.

The Zikrs mentioned in Canon Gairdner's articles are individual for the development of the spiritual life of those who become full members, but full members of the orders are very few compared to the vast numbers of lay members. For these there are corporate Zikrs, into which they are expected to put all their energy, books of instruction practically tell them that the more effort they exert in expelling the sounds and in swaying their bodies the greater the spiritual effect. Descriptions of such Zikrs are many and at least some of them should be read by the student, Vide Lane's *Modern Egyptians,* Ch. XXIV. pp. 438, 460, 450, 461 (1895 edition) Macdonald's *Aspects of Islam,* 159 et seq. (For the individual use of the Zikr see Macdonald's *The Religious Attitude and Life in Islam,* pp. 161, 259, 261, 274, 284-287). Hughes' *Dictionary of Islam* on "Zikr" pp. 703 to 710. An excellent impression of a Dimirdashija Zikr was written for the *Egyptian Gazette* some years ago and reprinted in *Blessed be Egypt,* 1912. After describing his entertainment by the Sheikh and the history of the order, the writer says :—

"Already the noise and din of many voices may be heard; we hurry out and stand upon chairs in the courtyard, Inside the mosque are seen the white forms of the disciples, about 200 in number, swaying to and fro in prayer. We take off our boots and mix with the praying peasant crowd outside. The sentiment of a common humanity thrills us. But unfortunately humanity does not smell very aromatic, so we hurry out again, and take our stand on the chairs once more. While the men pray inside we take the opportunity to obtain the following information.

Thirty days before the middle of the Hegira month, Shaban, disciples from every part of Islam send in their names as candidates for the retreat. During this period a candidate should eat nothing that has life. A College of 12 Sheikhs meanwhile assembles and decides on the list. There are only 65 cells, and so out of a list say of 500 applicants only 65 may be chosen. Age, piety and renown for good work are deciding factors in the final nominations. The Sayyed ed-Demerdachi enjoys the privilege of vetoing any name.

When the list is complete, successful candidates are informed and on Monday afternoon they arrive all ready for the retreat. In the evening they are treated to a huge dinner by their chief. After much prayer they are led to their various cells. These are small and bare of all furniture. Ventilation is provided for by a small slit in the door, no other arrangement being made for light.

During his three days' retreat, the candidate is not supposed to sleep a moment. To guard against human frailty a member of the College of twelve goes round the cells every thirty minutes and calls out "La ilaha-illalah". If the answer "Wa-Mohammed Rasûl allah" is not given back by the candidate, the door of the cell is thrown open and the anchorite is made to perform an ablution.

Coffee is served about eight times a night, with a glass of lemonade in the morning and a plate of rice cooked in oil in the evening. Except for this no food is given.

The ascetic is not supposed to talk to anyone or to see anyone during his retreat. If he goes out, it is with head and figure covered up. All muffled up and ghostlike the candidates glide out of their cells at noontide at the call of prayer. Then the retreat is resumed until the following day.

Thursday night ends this voluntary seclusion.

All of a sudden the undertone din of the worshippers rose to a shrill cry of "Allah, Allah, Allah." It was as if the whole group had suddenly become possessed with a wild zeal for God. No other word but Allah, Allah, was repeated again and again and yet again.

There is Sheikh Abd-el-Raheem, tall and towering above the rest. On his head he wears a huge green turban and the rest of his attire is pure white. His disciples too are all dressed in spotless white. Effective and Ghostlike. In a frenzy the holy name is uttered. It seemed as if the vocabulary had all been blotted out, and nothing but the word Allah was written on every page.

Is this the secret of the power of Islam?

And now the Sheikh and his disciples go to every cell door and bring out the occupant, and the only charm that is used, the only exhortation that is on every lip is the one great word "Allah, Allah, Allah". The weight of the word; the violence with which it beats upon the ear. It is like the echo of distant voices in the night; sounds from the sepulchral deeps of the everlasting sea. "Allah, Allah, Allah".

And now the great white company is complete, and the mosque is crowded again with their ghostlike forms. But they are no ghosts, these big and stalwart men who swing and sway to that magic name of Allah. We are ourselves becoming a part of it all, and are no longer oppressed, We have become affected, infected with this burning zeal. We would not have it cease, this soothing chant, retreating in the distance, echoing in the vaults and resounding in a hundred nooks and corners—"Allah, Allah, Allah."

The light has changed while we prayed. It is full moon. The Muezzin in the lofty minaret has ceased his song, and the faithful are in the secret sanctuary ranged in lines before the saint's tomb at Demerdache.

Two Christians enter and stand near the door behind this praying crowd in rows and rows, with their faces to the East where the sun rises. At first they hear a low murmuring of words that are not intelligible. Presently the murmur grows into a louder swell, that rises and falls like cadences of deep and distant music. Devotion and utter unconsciousness of our surroundings prevail everywhere. All eyes look to that one point in the inner sanctuary, the niche directly to the East.

And now the murmur grows louder, and suddenly bursting on the ear one hears the cry of the night "Allah-hu Akbar".

Though the sun shines bright outside, though the world is wide awake, the creation sings and laughs in the light of day, we close our eyes and listen, as the lulling word "Allah, Allah, Allah", is wafted across the kneeling, rising, bending crowd. Self is lost in soothing contemplation, and the last sounds we hear are the rising and falling cadences of the wonder working name of God.

5. *Places of Worship.* There was a time when monastic life was very strong amongst the dervishes, and from the end of the 13th century to almost the close of the Mameluke period we find monasteries built by many of the Sultans; the Arabic name for a Dervish monastery is "Khanka". Good specimens are to be seen at the mosque of Sultan Hassan and the tomb mosque of Sultan Barquq. Khanka on the main railway line bears that name because of a monastery built there by Baibars in gratitude for deliverance from a severe colic while out hunting on that spot.

Ibn Batuta, who visited Egypt in 1326, describes many of these and their strict rules, he states that the faqirs who inhabited them were chiefly Persian Sufis.

Later it seems that these were vetoed, except for foreign orders such as the Mawlawiya and the Bektashiya, and we have only to deal with the Zawias.

Nearly every order has its "Umm Zawiya", where the head of the order presides over regular performances of public Zikrs. This may be in a mosque or special building. Each order has many branch— Zawiyas, which are often of the simplest kind. Dupont and Coppolani say:— "In a word all places of a reunion of initiates in a brotherhood, all places where the derrer (teacher) is installed for teaching the Quran, wherever our Mohammedan brothers meet for prayer and give themselves to their mystical practices, are Zawiyas in contradistinction to mosques and Gawami' (Sing. Gami') consecrated and upheld by the temporal power and to which all believers have access". For further information on the Zawiyas read Dupont and Coppolani on the subject, pp. 204—208.

Another place of worship is the "Khilwa". This is for individua prayers, Zikrs and invocations of angels and saints. Any place where a devotee can be alone will serve this purpose providing it is ritually clean. It most not be thought that these Khilwas are only used by the more advanced Sufi; almost every dervish who aspires to become a Khalifa uses the Khilwa, and most dervish books give instructions for the ritual cleaning.

6. *Manazil*. Attention to worship leads the Murid on from stage to stage. These stages are called Manazil.

The different orders differently classify the stages of the journey that given by el-Nafasi is quoted in Hughes' *Dictionary of Islam*, p. 609.

El-Ubudiya service, the candidate is exhorted to a very strict observance of the law.

Ez-Zuhd, seclusion, the expelling of all desire from the heart.

El-Ma'arifa, knowledge, the gnosis or inner light.

El-Wagd, ecstacy.

El Haqiqa, truth, or the revelation of the very essence of the Godhead.

El-Wasl, union with God.

El Fana, total absorption into God, extinction.

Most systems give after El Fana, el Baqa as the final Manzil or stage, explaining it to be an abiding in God in the selfless man or of El Fana.

For Reading:

Hughes' *Dictionary of Islam*. Article "Faqir" p. 115. pp. 703-710

Sell's *Faith of Islam*, pp. 135-138.

Lane's *Modern Egyptians*, Chp. XXIV pp. 438, 450, 460, 461 (1895 edition)

Macdonald's, *Aspects of Islam*, pp. 159 to end of chapter.

Macdonald's *Religious Attitude*, pp. 161, 259, 261, 274, 284-28.

Moslem World Vol. II. Canon Gairdner's Articles entitled:— "The Way of a Mohammedan Mystic".

LECTURE V.

Saintship.

The whole tendency of all mysticisms, whether pagan, Moslem or Christian, is towards Saintship. When we say this, we do not shut our eyes to the fact that it is with the reputation for saintship that so many are concerned. Neither do we ignore the fact that the word "Saintship" can convey widely differing meanings and that the content of the word in the Christian revelation is totally different to that of all systems and even to the generally accepted ideas of Christian peoples. We therefore quote here at the outset of this lecture an illuminating interpretation of the Biblical teaching on Saintship by Dr. Dale in his comment on the opening words of St Paul's Epistle to the Ephesians, for it is most important to keep the true thought in view all the time we are studying the false conception of Sufism. Dr Dale says:

"They are 'saints'. It is impossible, I fear, to restore this word to its ancient and noble uses. It has been tainted with superstition, which has limited its application to those who have exhibited an exceptional holiness, and for many centuries it has been restricted to men whose holiness has been a very technical and artificial type. It has been degraded by unbelief which, in bitter mockery of the contrast between lofty aims and ignoble achievement, has flung it as an epithet of scorn at all who have professed to make the Divine will, and not the laws and customs of the human society, the rule of their conduct. In the early days all Christians were 'saints'. The title did not attribute any personal merit to them; it simply recalled their prerogatives and their obligations. When however they were so described they were reminded that God had made them His own. They were 'holy' because they belonged to him. The temple had once been 'holy', not because of its magnitude, its stateliness, and the costly materials of which it was built, but because it was the home of God; and the tabernacle which was erected in the wilderness, though a much meaner structure, was just as 'holy' as the temple of Solomon, with its marble courts, and its profusion of cedar and brass and silver and gold. The altars were 'holy' because they were erected for the service of God. The sacrifices were 'holy' because they were offered to Him. The Priests were 'holy' because they were divinely chosen to discharge the functions of the temple service. The Sabbath was 'holy' because God had placed His hand upon it and separated its hours from common uses. The whole Jewish people were 'holy' because they were organized into a nation, and not for common purposes which have been the ends of the national existence of other races, but to receive in trust for all mankind exceptional revelations of the character and will of God. And now, according to Paul's conception, every Christian man was a temple, a sacrifice, a priest; his whole life was a Sabbath; he belonged to an elect race; he was the subject of an invisible and Divine Kingdom; he was a 'saint'.

"The institutions of Judaism had given only a very rough and coarse representation of the idea of holiness; and there are passages in this epistle which will throw far more light upon what is really meant by being a 'Saint' than we can derive from the Jewish temple, and the Jewish priests, the sacrifices and the Jewish sabbath; but the rudimentary conception is to be found in the holy places, the holy things, the holy times, and the holy persons of the ancient faith.

"And there was one essential element in that rudimentary conception which remains unchanged in the new and higher form of sanctity which is presented in the Christian Church. Speaking broadly, nothing became 'holy' in Jewish times by any human act consecrating it to God. No man could erect a building and make it a temple. There was one temple only, and this had been erected by Divine appointment and Divine plan. When the Jews began to build synagogues in different parts of the country for religious instruction and worship, it was not supposed that the buildings had any sanctity. A synagogue was not, like the temple, the home and place of God; it was erected for the convenience of a congregation. Nor could any man at the impulse of his own devout zeal, make himself a priest, or obtain admission to the priesthood by the authority of those who were priests already. No man took this honour to himself; it belonged exclusively to the family on which God had conferred it. Nor could any general consent to set apart a day for religious uses make the day sacred as the Sabbath was sacred. No person, no place, no time, could be set apart for God by any human appointment and so made holy. Every consecrated person, place and time was consecrated, not by the fervour of human devotion, but by the authority of the Divine will. And a 'Saint', a consecrated man, according to the apostolic conception, is one whom God has set apart for Himself. The act of consecrating is God's act not ours. As I have said already, the title of 'saint' implies not personal merit; it is the record of a great manifestation of God's condescension and love. Our part is subordinate and secondary. We have only to submit to the authority of the Divine claim, and to receive the dignity conferred by the Divine love. The common conception is precisely the reverse of this, and the reverse of the truth. It begins with a human volition instead of a Divine volition. It makes the act of consecration a human act instead of a divine act. God's place becomes subordinate and secondary. He only accepts what we give. As the sanctity is supposed to originate in the voluntary surrender of the heart and life to God, the measure of the sanctity is determined by the extent of surrender ; and a man is more or less a saint in the degree in which he makes himself over to God.

"The apostolic idea was far more profound. It was an essential part of Paul's whole theory of man's relation to God. The theology of the Epistle to the Romans, the theology of this Epistle, obliged him to rest the idea of sanctity, not on the shifting sands of human volition, but on the eternal foundations of the Divine love."

1. Miss Gregory in her little book *Christian Mysticism* to which we have already referred, in grouping mystics, quotes Vaughan's threefold division : the theopathetic ; the theosophic, and the theurgic ; or, as she says "to put it into more comprehensible language, the saint, the sage, and the spiritualist". We would replace her last word by "the wielder of spiritual forces". The dervish Wali or saint nearly always combines all three characteristics ; though as a rule one is outstanding. In Arabic we read of (a) "*Manaqib el-Wali*" meaning, that which is known of the excellency of his disposition and character ; this would be the theopathetic sainthood. Then of (b) "*Karamat el Wali*" meaning the honours God has bestowed upon the saint in enabling him to perform wonders ; this would be theurgic sainthood. Then of (c) "*Ulum el Wali*" meaning the intuitive knowledge bestowed upon him ; this would be the theosophic side of sainthood. Abu Yazid el Bastami said to the learned men of his day. "You have taken your knowledge from the scholastic theologian, the dead from the dead ; we have taken our knowledge from the Living One."

A few examples of these may be taken from *Ma'athir el Shadhaliya* though it must be understood that Dervish books on sale in every market place in Egypt teem with instances, and the minds of the masses of the people who cannot read dwell very largely on such things.

(a) When Abu Hassan-el-Shadhali arrived at the stage of death to all desire for six months he remained silent not daring to ask God for anything. Then a voice within him cried "Ask for a worship that does not vascillate between God's gifts and His withholdings". "So" he said, "I asked God for it obediently, not disallowing that which God had granted, for verily he created whatsoever He wills and with him is no preference."

(b) When el-Shadhali was travelling eastward to Egypt an enemy sent letters before him to the Sultan warning him that el-Shadhali would pollute Egypt as he had done Tunis. On arrival at Alexandria, strict orders were given that he was to be confined to that city, no reason being given. The Sultan had at this time levied a tax on some Sheikhs of a village called Kabaa. When they heard of the arrival of el Shadhali they came to ask the benefit of his prayers. He promised to go to Cairo and petition the Sultan on their behalf. The story then goes on to relate how they went through the "Bab Sidra Gate" without being seen, though there was stationed there a Government Post which vigorously searched all who went in and out. When they arrived at the citadel of Cairo, and entered the palace of the Sultan, he refused to hear the petition, saying that the Sheikh had need to petition on behalf of himself and showed him his enemy's (Ibn el-Bara's) communication. The Sheikh briefly replied that he, the Sultan, and Ibn el-Bara were in God's hands, and he left his presence. Immediately after he had left, the judges asked a question of the Sultan but he made no sign ; they shook him and he was as dead. In great haste they went after the Sheikh and humbly besought his return. On returning he shook the Sultan with his blessed hand and he was restored and he descended from the throne, made his obeisance to the Sheikh, gave him all his requests, and made him come to the Citadel as his guest. This is one of the least strange of the Karamat.

(c) It is said of him that he used to speak by intuitive light about hidden things ; in addition he was learned about the outward sciences of religion and literature; yet it was the gift of the inward light that brought him disciples from all parts. The book itself is largely given over to this teaching which came from the inner light.

2. We have been thinking so far of saints as they are set forth in the literature of Dervishism. Let us now consider what they are actually. The vileness of these men, who pose as living saints, has not infrequently been the theme, not of missionaries who are generally considered prejudiced and iconoclastic, but of Orientalists and even of Moslem writers. Nevertheless in the most degenerate days there are always some who have a better claim to being honoured as saints on account of their abstemious practices, their real life of meditation and their sincere desire to fulfill all righteousness as they understand it.

It is a delight to meet such characters and quietly to converse with them, if one can avoid the stereotyped form of controversy as to the respective merits of Christianity and Islam, into which they will constantly try to enter. But these men are few and far between ; you may come across them in little shops in the native bazaars, or plaiting baskets from the sharp lance like leaves of the palm trees in the open street of some village (a sincere repentance is named after this particular craft, taubet el-khaws, which was also a mark of the ascetic life amongst the monks of the Nitrian desert).

Then there is a very large class whose reputation for saintship depends upon their reputation for magical powers; this includes almost all Khalifas of the Dervish Orders. Lastly all form of madness and idiocy, excepting that attributed to jinn-possession, are attributed to God having so favoured the afflicted one that He has taken his mind away to heaven, there to gaze upon the preserved tablet of revelation, whilst his grosser parts remain here in the world of men, hence they are saints. Lane was not far wrong when he said. "Most of the reputed saints of Egypt are either lunatics or idiots or imposters".

The student must recall here the incident previously referred to of the meeting of Moses and El-Khidr. and that passage in Lane's *Modern Egyptians* built on this Koranic passage, and realize what it must mean that no saint can be judged by any moral standard. Think, too, that these men specially appeal to the women of Islam and have access into their houses in a way impossible to other men, and at once you will get something of a picture of the awful possibilities of this system, but your picture will most probably be far from the vile reality.

In concluding this paragraph we must quote from Prof. Nicholson's *The Mystics of Islam.* "Neither deep learning in divinity nor devotion to good works, nor asceticism, nor moral purity makes the Mohammedan a saint; he may have all or none of these things, but the only indispensable qualification is that ecstasy and rapture which is the outward sign of 'passing away' from the phenomenal self. Anyone thus enraptured is a wali, and when such persons are recognized through their power of working miracles they are venerated after death and also during their lives. The Mohammedan's notion of the saint as a person possessed by God allows a very wide application of the term, in popular usage it extends from the greates Sufi theosophists like Jalaluddin Rumi and Ibn el-'Arabi down to those who have gained sanctity only by losing sanity; victims of epilepsy and hysteria, half witted idiots and harmless lunatics". I am well aware that in this chapter scant justice has been done to a great subject. The historian of Sufism must acknowledge, however he may deplore, the fundamental influence which it has exerted in its practical results, grovelling submission to the authority of an ecstatic class of men, dependence on their favour, pilgrimages to their shrines, adoration of their relics, devotion of every mental and spiritual faculty to their service. It may be dangerous to worship God by one's own inner light, but it is far more deadly to seek Him by the inner light of another. Vicarious holiness has no compensation.

3. References have already been made to the mad saints; something further must be said. A convert from Islam who had been an Azharite Sheikh and a former pupil of Mohammed Abdu, one of the most advanced teachers, and he himself very antagonistic to superstition, was asked what was his judgement with regard to mad Saints. He said the Azhar carefully distinguished between the "Magnun" (mad because possessed of a Jinn) and the "Magzub (the attracted of God) But with regard to the Magzub they considered that these men as a class held first rank as saints and they based their belief on the following well founded tradition of the prophet. "The ignorant Salik is nearer to God than the learned Salik, and will take precedence over him in the day of judgement" (Sahih el-Bukhari).

This man being an Egyptian would most certainly be referring, to a mad saint, but a reference to Hughes' *Dictionary of Islam* p. 612, will show that Indian Moslem thought, which Hughes' *Dictionary* especially reflects, has a more exalted conception of the Magzub, and this more exalted thought may have been the influencing one on the Azhar teaching in early days.

4. How does a Moslem become a Saint? Shakespeare gives us the answer concisely: "Some are born great, some achieve greatness, some have greatness thrust upon them". Very literally some are born saints; take for example the Sayyids of the Mirghaniya order.

It would seem that every member of the leading family in direct line of descent from the founder is considered a saint. Others seem to be born with a natural aptitude for religious attainment. Some others by a strict observance of all ascetic practices prescribed by their Sheikhs and by much meditation, prayer and use of the Zikr honestly arrive at a reputation for saintliness; by far the greater part have this reputation as their goal and arrive there by many devious courses, generally by simulating ecstatic experiences or by the practice of magic. Very occasionally the greatness is thrust upon them, such as the instance mentioned in a previous chapter when returned pilgrims from Mecca swore to having met and talked with a local man in the Haram when it was known that he had never left his native town.

Finally it behoves us as missionaries, to combat this idea of saintship which holds the people in such grips. We must find out if we ourselves are quite clear as to what constitutes saintship Not only so, but we must remember that we too are called to be saints. This the missionary is apt to forget in the great pressure of work that shorthandedness and a vast field involve. We are to demonstrate practically that what the law could not do in that it was weak through the flesh, God, by sending His own Son, can do in us, so that our righteousness shall exceed the righteousness of the Scribes and Pharisees. Our standards of righteousness can only be the righteousness of God, When we say He is righteous we mean that all His acts are in conformity with His nature. Our standard of holiness will therefore increase with the increase of our knowledge of God's nature at which we can arrive, not by an uncertain inner light but by God's great revelation of Himself in our Lord Jesus Christ.

We must ever be on the watch against the foolishness of the Galatians, whilst at the same time we must remember that holiness by faith comes not to him who does not hunger and thirst after righteousness. Again I would urge that it is in the subject of saintship we have the crux of the problem of Islam's hold upon the masses, and mere theorists as to right views of saintship will not successfully combat their errors. We are called to be saints.

For Reading :—
    Macdonald's *The Religious Attitude and Life in Islam*,
        Lectures VI & VII & IX,

LECTURE VI.
Magic.

Magic plays a most important part in the Dervish system. It has always been an integral part of Islam but has been highly developed by the Dervish Orders who have borrowed from every system of mysticism known in the Orient.

1. Egypt as a Source. In Dr. Budge's *Short History of the Egyptian People,* he has a chapter on "Egyptian Magic and Religion" which is most interesting reading. We would here, however, quote a very few sentences from that Chapter.

"However far back we go we find magic flourishing side by side with religion. Be this as it may, there were at all times in use in Egypt two kinds of magic, the one lawful and the other unlawful, or, as we say to day "White Magic" and "Black Magic". The two greatest men in Egypt were the King and the Magician (the Medicine man or Witch Doctor of the modern African peoples)...

"The title of this great magician was "Khen-heb", and his power was very great. He knew all the words and names of power, he composed spells, he cast out devils, he sent dreams to sleeping folk and interpreted dreams, he produced and stilled storms, he foretold the future, he raised the dead, he laid ghosts, he possessed the secret of reciting the words of the liturgy in such a way that material offering became changed into the spirit food of the Gods. He was of necessity a learned man, and he knew the magical and religious literature thoroughly; and of course he could write; these abilities commanded the respect and fear of the people to whom the written word was always sacred......

"Having by some means found out the secret or 'hidden' name of a particular god or friend, he addressed this being by that name, then adjured him to do his will...... In all such spells or adjurations names of power play a very prominent part. It was impossible for a Magician to live in every tomb to protect every mummy, but he claimed to protect them by written spells.... Theban and Saite Rescensions of the *Book of the Dead* are full of spells accompanied by magic drawings. Thus the chapter of the Ladder and the drawing of it would secure for the deceased the use of the famous ladder, whereby Osiris had climbed up from earth to heaven. The chapter of the Ferry boat and the picture of it would provide a boat for the deceased when he desired to sail across the Nile to the other world. Besides magical names and magical drawings, the Khen-heb used freely magical figures made of various substances, but especially in wax, for trasmitting good and evil, to the living and the dead. From Egypt the use of magical figures passed to the continent of

Europe and thus to England...... Besides spells, magical drawings and magical figures, the magician was called upon to *provide amulets* for the living who wished to carry about with them the protection of the gods, spirits and deceased animals, and to benefit by their power, and also for the dead."

In the midst of a description of these amulets Dr, Budge describes the one so-well known to all dwellers on the Nile: "The *scarab* or *beetle*, the symbol of new life and virility and resurrection was associated with god Khepera, Kheperr i.e. the 'Roller' who rolled the ball of the sun across the sky. Having prepared a ball of matter to serve as food to its off spring, the female beetle rolled it into a hole in the ground in which it had laid one egg, and when the young beetle was hatched out it fed upon it. With this egg was associated the idea of 'only begotten' and the beetle gave to the wearer the protection of the only begotten son of the primeval God...."

"The Khen-heb was in early times also a physician, and as he administered his medicines to the patient he assisted their operation by reciting spells, charms and incantations, and sometimes by performing ceremonies...." A sharp distinction must be drawn between magicians of this class and the astrologers, soothsayers, fortune tellers, necromancers, casters of nativities, and sorcerers of all kinds who flourished in Egypt from the reign of Rameses II and onwards.

"The latter class of physicians were imposters who deceived the people and professed to read the future by the help of absurd tricks and ceremonies, to foretell dreams, to transform men into animals and reptiles, to heal the sick, to bring the spirits of the dead back to this earth, to work miracles by means of potions derived from the bodies of the dead, and to be able to make amulets that would protect their owners for ever against every hostile creature or thing in this world or the next. Such men only flourished in Egypt when her people as a whole had lost their belief in Osiris and the other ancient gods, and were seeking to make debased superstition take its place".

Every word of this can be paralleled in the magic practised in Egypt by the Dervish orders, especially the last paragraph and Maspero tells us in his *New Light on Ancient Egypt* that in the first century A.D. all the systems of magic extant were combined.

2. *Judaism as a source*. Probably most of the ancient Egyptian magic came to Dervishism through Judaism, though undoubtedly much would live on in the country down through the ages. Nearly all references to magic and magicians in the Old Testament have a connection with Egypt. The Jews borrowed and developed the magic of Egypt. The Talmud is a perfect mine of magical formulae. The "Shems-el-Maʻârif" an Arabic book of magic, very

widely sold, has many traces of this Jewish source. Jewish names for God such as El, Jah, Elohim, &c., and quite a large a number of Jewish names for angels.

3. The Effect of Magic. The student must read in Lane's *Modern Egyptians,* chapter XII and Mr. Hayes' article in in the *Moslem World* 1914, to get an impression of the evil effects the practice of magic has upon the common people. Dr. Zwemer's *Animism in Islam,* will also greatly help to an appreciation of its widespread and sinister hold. The article on magic in Hughes' *Dictionary of Islam.* should be read and the article Da'wah should be glanced through. Macdonald's *Aspects of Islam* pp. 336 to 334 should be read. Very interesting reading is also to be found in his *The Religious Attitude and Life in Islam,* pp. 15, 112, 114-116, 126, 128.

4. The Moroccan Mohammedans. Place as much emphasis on magic and practice it so widely and freely, that in this country the word "Maghraby" is synonymous with Magician. The making of amulets and divination by sand is almost wholly in the hands of natives of Darfur who also are experts in other forms of magic. If the student desires to get an idea of how prevalent are the practices of magic let him go in and out of any village in Egypt and notice, for example, as only one of many methods of avoiding evil the number of houses that have pieces of rag tied somewhere to the bars of their lower windows. It will be easier, however, to count those that are devoid of rags.

For Reading:—
Lane's *Modern Egyptians* Chap. XII.
Macdonald's *Aspects of Islam,* pp. 536-344.
    do   *Religious Life and Attitude,* pp. 51, 122, 114-125, 128.
Hayes' Article in *The Moslem World,* October 1914.

www.ingramcontent.com/pod-product-compliance
Lightning Source LLC
Chambersburg PA
CBHW031639160426
43196CB00006B/486